My Son Dave (the Duck)
A Story About Loving and Letting Go

Written By Plynn Gutman
Illustrated by Jessica Lynn Woodson

For my son, Dave, wherever you are.

Table of Contents

Chapter One

Derivation

It was a disquieting epiphany, the realization that my sons were growing up.

This came to me one New Years day. My husband Mike and our teenage sons, Mitch and Dan, were lounging around, watching a football game. I stood next to the counter that separated the kitchen from the family room, staring at them, doing an inventory of the year's events and found myself yearning for times past. Times when these boys, now becoming young men, hung on my every word – when Mitch begged me to play Monopoly with him at night before bed, or Dan wanted to hold my hand while we drove in the car. A deep sadness plunked itself in the core of my being.

It seemed, as if by instinct, they were pulling away from me. I could say I knew this day was coming, that I was prepared and excited to watch them walk into adulthood. I think I fooled myself into believing I was. But I wasn't. As they sat there together commenting back and forth about the game in husky man-voices, I wanted to call out, "No, don't go! I'll play cars with you, a board game, anything – just don't leave."

Once, I had a romantic vision of how I would cut those symbolic apron strings. Like an old movie, there at the train station my sons would stand, caps in hand, tears in their eyes, saying, "Mom, we don't want to leave you. Please let us stay." And I would say in a solemn monologue, "No, my sons. It is time for you to go. You must find your own ways in the world. Don't worry about me. I'll be fine. Now go, the conductor is waiting for you." Then, with desperate waves from the open window, they would leave, the lonely howl of the train whistle crying out their departure. And I would blow them brave kisses from the platform and dab away my tears with a lace handkerchief, my head nestled in my husband's broad chest.

It's odd to think that this one football game could be pulling my sons from my world and jettisoning them into another. But there are points in time – change points – when a light goes on somewhere inside, and you know that something has shifted. You know you can't go back. At that moment I realized that I was at the beginning of the end of a piece of my life, and it made me want to cry.

I decided to go for a walk to settle myself. The sky was clear, the air barely crisp: January in Arizona. I walked, passing homes of this friend of Mitch's and that friend of

Dan's. I could hear sounds of laughter through open windows and smell meat grilling on backyard barbeques as I muttered down the street in a blur of tears. And then I saw it – the tiny, brown head of a bird along the sidewalk curb ahead of me. I wiped my eyes and quickened my pace to catch up to the bobbling head. It scurried into the middle of the road. Like a movie in fast forward, its body waddled back and forth on miniature, webbed feet the color of Sunkist oranges. I gasped, covering my mouth with my hand to stifle an involuntary giggle. A baby duck at this time of year? In this suburban neighborhood? I darted my head around, looking for someone or something to confirm the feathered illusion. But we were alone: this little, brown bird and me.

Bent in an awkward frog-like position I followed the duckling, gently scooped it up and headed straight for home.

"You will not believe what I just found," I said as I slowly opened my hands. When the tiny head with its muddy orange beak peeked out my sons' faces softened, their eyes widened.

"What should we call him?" the old Monopoly excitement buzzed in Mitch's voice.

"Dave is the first name that comes to my mind. What do you think?"

"Dave the Duck," Mitch grinned.

"It's good, Mom," Dan said. "Can I hold him?" He nestled the downy body close to his cheek. "I wonder if he's hungry?"

Only Dan, my bottomless pit, would think of food first. I had no idea what a duck should eat. I had no idea how to care for it, period. Maybe we could try baby cereal, which I always kept in the cupboard in case a stray kitten showed up at our doorstep.

Our house seemed to be posted with a neon sign, reading "Lost Animals Welcome." Over the years numerous cats and dogs had taken refuge with us until their owners could be found. Our most recent ward was a large, white and black rabbit. Six months prior, Dan had found him nibbling on the petunias in our front yard. After I made him comb the neighborhood for the bunny's owner, Dan returned with no claim on the creature, a donated bag of rabbit food and a big grin on his face. So Speedy, as we called him, stayed, sharing our backyard with a desert tortoise we found several years ago trying to make its way across a busy street.

I enjoyed our wayward visitors, and the boys seemed to relish the heroic purpose of our rescues, but my husband always grumbled, "We're not the local animal shelter, you know." But Dave was different. "We're going to have to find something to keep him in at night so he feels safe," Mike said.

The next few hours were a flurry of activity as we took turns holding the new baby while others searched for items that would make him feel comfortable and at home. The boys were all giggles and animated gawkiness, and for a moment I was transported back in time to what once had been.

By early evening we had created a home for Dave in a small, plastic lizard cage, once inhabited by our gecko, Ernie, who had gone on to lizard heaven some time ago. We covered its floor with a face towel, bunched to form a pillow. Cream of wheat granules mixed with warm water and bits of grass would do until we could find real duck food.

Crouched on the kitchen floor like campers around a fire, we watched Dave attempt to eat. I nudged his head toward the bowl to touch his bill to the cereal. After a few tries he began to chomp, chomp, chomp, then lift his head and shake it vigorously back and forth, spewing the mush in all directions. We leaned back in unison to avoid the spray, laughing and covering our faces.

By the time he finished eating, his brown body was speckled white with bits of cereal, so we put him in a salad bowl of water for a bath. Around and around he swam, those fruit-colored flippers pedaling in two-four time. Every so often he dipped his head into the water and then pulled up quickly, making a shower of droplets run down his back, all the while quacking, soft and low.

I gingerly lifted him out of the water into a hand towel and set him on my lap where he shook and fluffed his feathers, and preened his puny chest. I decided it was Dave's bedtime, so the boys said their goodnights and moved on to do their homework and other on-the-verge-of manly things.

I sat alone on the floor by his cage in the corner of our family room holding him, swathed in a face towel, close to my body. He snuggled his bill between my index and middle fingers, and I stroked his head with my thumb. Slowly his eyes quivered into closing. Ever so gently I moved to lay him in his cage.

"In tonight's news …!" The volume on the television seemed to shoot up the decibel scale. Dave shuddered to attention.

"Michael," I hissed, "turn that thing down. I'm trying to the put the duck to sleep."

"Sorry, I'll go watch it in the bedroom."

"It's okay little one, Daddy didn't mean to scare you," I crooned.

As Dave, once again, nestled in, his bill warm between my fingers, my mind flooded with memories of motherhood. I thought of sleepless nights and fevers and flu, of T-ball games and Taekwondo lessons, of snuggles and kisses on sweaty little-boy heads until the duck fell asleep.

Chapter Two
Adaptation

I shuffled around the kitchen, Frankenstein-style.

Dave was tucked in at the side of my neck – a place he loved to be – held there by a large, orange and cream paisley scarf I had wrapped around my head, fashioned after a hijab but loose and messy. I found that scarf in the bowels of my closet, a memento I had kept from my younger days. One of those items that tracks your history, popping up in photos again and again – first in my teens as a halter top, triangled, tied around my neck and knotted behind my back; then in my disco days, covering my hair as a bandana, paired with large gold hoop earrings and false eyelashes; and again later in various forms, my vain attempts to follow the directions from a women's magazine article that promised twenty fantastic ways to make it the ultimate fashion accessory. After that I was too busy with two toddlers and had no time or patience for such things. Of course, it popped up again once or twice, as part of a pirate costume on Halloween, but for the most part the orange and cream paisley scarf lay dormant until the duck came into my life.

Dave had adopted me as his mother, following me everywhere, making throaty quacks with every wobble. His tiny stature kept him in constant danger of being stepped on, so I tried to devise a carrying contraption that soothed his need to be near me. Nestled in at the back of my neck like a lumpy growth protruding from the scarf, he would sleep, downy and warm. I looked ridiculous. But mothers make these kinds of sacrifices.

Once, when I passed my reflection in the window I stopped, stared and wondered why I was going to such great lengths to comfort a duck. Then, in his child-like curiosity, he poked his head out the side of the scarf by the nape of my neck. He reminded me of Dan peeking over my shoulder, nestled in the baby backpack, all those years ago. I smiled and moved on.

But the headdress didn't last. My neck was sore from staying rigid for long periods of time. And, whenever I bent forward I was afraid he would fall out of the makeshift carriage. Finally, I came up with something that suited both Dave and me. I wore a long sweater that covered my bottom and had a button-up front with a V-opening to the navel. Then I tied my paisley scarf tight around my waist, which provided Dave with a roomy new mobile home inside the sweater. The knit material expanded as he maneuvered around the length of my waist with the scarf acting as a shelf. He could sleep in various locations or poke his head out the front of the V to view his surroundings in relative safety.

During those first weeks, Dave and I spent almost every waking moment together. Our bonding soothed me, tucking that sadness away. I even took him on errands with me in the car. He sat in a small towel on my lap while I drove, occasionally looking up at me with one beady eye as if wanting assurance that all was right with our world, making a guttural sound like a tiny engine humming behind his bill.

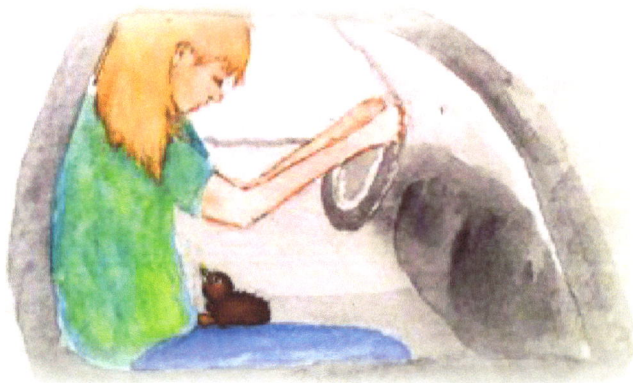

I easily understood the duck's voice and habits. In my family, I was the youngest of five children and lived on a remote farm in southern Saskatchewan. My closest sibling was a boy and five years older than I, so animals were my early companions. I learned to watch the way an animal looked at me when I talked to it: its eyes focused, returning a silent response or using its voice with different tones and inflections to say hello or tell me it was time for dinner or bed.

I enjoyed Dave's company, but by evening I was often weary from his constant care and called on my family to share duck duty. The boys were good about helping, intrigued by the idea of having a baby brother, even if it was a duck. But Dave's favorite family member, next to me, was my husband.

After dinner, when Mike sat in his recliner to relax and watch some television, I placed the duck on his lap, "Okay, Dad, it's your turn with the baby."

He cupped his bear paw hands around Dave and held him next to his stomach. Spying a neck to cuddle, the duckling made his way up Mike's chest in a strained waddle to sit on his shoulder where he promptly began to preen my husband's beard, working his way to his mustache. Mike shivered and groaned between pursed lips, "Does he have to do that?"

"Don't wiggle, Michael. He'll lose his balance. He's just showing you that he loves you."

After five or ten minutes of intense grooming that left my husband's beard looking unkempt and his mustache askew, Dave's eyelids began to flutter from fatigue. He wobbled into the crevice between the chair and Mike's shoulder, tucked his beak into the soft curls at the back of his adopted dad's head, and chattering his own lullaby, fell asleep. Eventually Mike got used to their routine. He, too, would fall asleep, his head rolled toward the duckling making a cozy nest with his hair, his soft snore singing harmony with Dave's whispering quack.

Dave changed with each passing day. His neck got longer and his feet bigger. Lanky with mussed up feathers, he looked like a teenager. Soon his plastic salad-bowl-bathtub had to be replaced by my giant bread-making bowl, and his hand-me-down lizard cage exchanged for a large wire one we found tucked away in our shed. And when he wasn't perched in one of our laps, he had the run of the kitchen and family room, both with tiled floors that made cleaning up his duck messes an easy task.

One evening I noticed Dave crouched next to the brass, wood holder by the fireplace, looking at his reflection in the yellow metal and making the low, guttural sounds, which signified that bedtime was near. He reminded me of a parakeet I had as a child; it would sit and look at the mirror in its cage and coo itself to sleep. I thought that Dave might be doing the same thing.

"Mike, do we still have that old bathroom mirror stored somewhere?"

"Yeah, I think so." He had that what-now tone to his voice.

"I think Dave would like that mirror in his cage. It might help him settle in at night, like he has another duck in there with him."

"You're weird."

"Please. Let's just try it."

With a huff and a puff and a flashlight my husband indulged me, rummaged through the shed until he found the mirror and put it against the wall behind Dave's cage.

Later, while Mike watched the news on low volume and the boys were tending to their homework, I sat on the floor in front of the duck-bedroom. Dave had finished his bath and I was putting him to sleep in the usual manner – his warm body next to my belly with his bill snuggled between the fingers of one hand while my other held him close and fondled the soft flesh of his webbed feet. I smiled at our reflection in his new mirror.

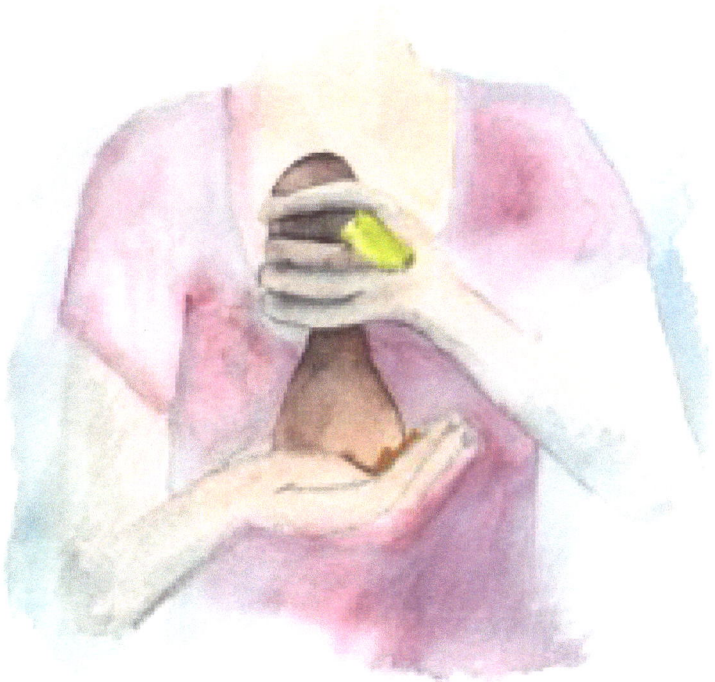

I laid him carefully in his cage. He shuffled on his belly toward the mirror and began to sing his low, gravelly lullaby to his reflection. Then I waited as I once would have with Dan – such a busy little boy, sometimes too restless to sleep – perched on the edge of his bed, watching him until his dreams carried him to rest.

I watched and waited until my duck was quiet and his eyes closed.

Chapter Three
Evolution

As Dave continued to grow, so did his messes.

The poop was taking its toll on all of us. Everyone walked head down, scouting the tile for his muddy surprises. A bottle of Windex and a roll of paper towels had a permanent place on the kitchen counter, ready for the inevitable. Mitch and Dan were gracious about cleaning up after Dave but Mike, who was never good about baby poop, would just shudder and point, "He did it again, Plynn."

We all agreed that Dave needed more space so I moved his home to the backyard patio next to the house. With his mirror propped at the back of the cage, I replaced his face-towel bed with a larger bath towel and draped an old blanket over the top and sides of the cage for protection against wind. It looked like a miniature, hobo house, make-shift but useable.

A tub, which Mike brought home from work that had once been used to mix construction materials, now became our duck's new bath. The boys made a small ramp with bricks and pieces of wood for Dave to get in and out of his tub, and I taught him to walk it by feeding him little bits of cornflakes along the way. There were two things Dave loved besides attending to Mike's beard: water and cornflakes. So within a couple of days he had the wooden route mastered.

He spent hours swimming and dipping, and then tumbled out of the water onto the ramp where he fluffed and preened until his feathers looked like a dandelion puff.

The outdoors brought Dave new freedom and a new friend. Speedy, our rabbit, became his playmate. Dave followed the rabbit around the yard, quacking as if he was scolding him for some indiscretion until Speedy stopped and hunched down. Then Dave would begin to groom his fur. The more the duck preened the more the rabbit relaxed, head low to the ground, eyes closed, until his hind legs splayed behind him.

Over time Dave got too big to take in the car. His rounding body no longer fit comfortably between the steering wheel and me. And though he came in the house to visit,

I decided to encourage him to stay outdoors because of the poop problem. So Dave and I began to spend our time together in the backyard. Every day we had the same routine. I would sit on a patio chair and call his name, "Dave, Dave," with a little up and down swing on the intonation of the "a." Even if he was in my sight, I called him. It was part of the ceremony. He would walk toward me, his tail feathers dipping and swaying back and forth, and talk to me, "Wwraaack, wwrack, wwrack," soft and low like he was saying, "Where have you been? I've been waiting for you."

I replied in his language as closely as I could imitate and then, with a cornflake between my lips, bent forward to meet his long, beaked face. Dave would pluck the food from my mouth in a whisper of a kiss.

"Good boy," I'd say, then pat my lap and gently lift him to sit on me. With a wiggle he would settle into the dip between my legs and eat the rest of the cornflakes from my hand while I stroked the silky feathers of his back. As time went on, all I had to do was pat my lap and he would flutter up and nestle in.

Dave was changing before my eyes. I suspected that he was a Mallard but as his clay brown feathers began to darken and speckle, I was certain. For almost a week his coloring seemed that of a female, but then in a quantum moment Dave assured me of his maleness by sprouting curly, white tail feathers while a ring of the same brilliance began to form around his neck. Daily, iridescent, emerald green feathers replaced the brown ones on his head, starting at his beak and working their way slowly, as if one by one, to that emerging white ring. He reminded me of Mitch, whose sprouting whiskers were also changing the landscape of his face.

In the midst of this evolution, Dave had an awakening. For several weeks he had navigated our large backyard, nibbling on plants, pooping here and there, and waddling after Speedy, playing their grooming game, all without taking notice of the grand, kidney-shaped body of shimmering liquid: our swimming pool. Then one day – just a regular duck day – he simply plopped off its edge into the water, swimming quickly and quacking in a happy refrain that seemed to say, "Oh-my-oh-my-oh-my-look-what-I-found."

One cloudless, spring afternoon I joined Dave in the backyard for our daily ritual. He was standing at the far end of the pool quietly guarding his domain. I noticed how broad he was becoming, how the dark, almost-black feathers of his body looked like satin in the sun. He stretched his neck forward and looked in my direction as I sat down and called his name, "Dave, Dave." I expected him to plunk into the water and swim across the pool to me, which was his preference to walking now. Instead, in one fluid, slow motion, he opened his wings, revealing cloud-white feathers striped with metallic, royal blue, and flew in a gentle swoop across the pool towards me. He settled in an audible flutter on the patio, barely three feet from my chair. As he approached me it appeared as if his baby waddle had transformed into a confident strut, his "Wwraaak, wwraak, wwrack," proud, mature.

I could not return his greeting. My astonishment had stuffed itself deep into my throat. Dave had evolved into an elegant, male Mallard in what seemed like only a moment.

Chapter Four
Exploration

The April air held that beckoning scent of gathered flowers as the sun sprawled in the clear, morning sky.

It had been almost four months since I'd found Dave.

I sat on the patio chair sipping coffee. Speedy nibbled on weeds sprouting sporadically in the landscape, and Mike stood next to the pool, head down, in what appeared to be deep thought. Dave was next to him, neck long and regal. It was an odd sight. Instead of a man and his dog, it was a man and his duck.

"What are you doing, Mike?"

"I'm looking at the mess Dave has made of the pool."

As if on cue Dave plopped in the water and blopped a

nice, big poop that floated willy-nilly to the bottom.

"I don't know if the stains will come out of the plaster, Plynn."

Dave paddled around the pool, dipping his head in the water and then pulling it out quickly, splashing droplets on his back feathers, just like he did that very first night in his salad-bowl-tub. He muttered a continuous, low quack as he swam.

Mike got a long-handled brush from the storage shed and began to whisk the bottom of the pool in a furious motion that reminded me of plunging a toilet. Dave bobbed up and down in the wake. "Well, it looks like we're going to have to empty the pool and acid wash the plaster. The brush isn't touching these stains."

Mike loves his pool. Normally by April he would already be taking a morning dip to start the day, hooting in its invigorating freshness, goose bumps from head to toe. With the water warming and summer in sight, I knew something had to be done. We discussed building a duck pond in our ample yard, but both knew I could never get Dave to give

up possession of the pool. And even if I could, his wings would have to be clipped so that he would stay in the yard, or I'd need to be prepared to deal with the possibility of a multitude of mallards coming home with Dave to live with us. The birds I could handle; the multitudinous messes, I could not.

There was no easy answer.

We finally agreed that I would find Dave a safe place to live, in freedom and with his own kind. Over several weeks that followed I began to explore every lake, pond and park in the area. At the same time, Dave began some exploration of his own. He started to leave the yard on flying expeditions. I was as nervous as the times the boys went on their first sleepovers. To make matters worse, he didn't know how to navigate his landings into our back-yard, which was filled with towering pine trees. And I had no way to teach him.

I arrived home one day to find him squatted stoically in the courtyard by our front door.

When I got out of the car Dave waddled toward me, neck stretched out and quacking loudly, as if to say, "Where-have-you-been-I-can't-get-in!" He followed me into the house, out the rear door to the yard, still squawking, and went straight to the pool. He slid in and puddled along making his mutter-quack of contentment. I had to wonder if, in the end, our bond would put Dave in harm's way. What did he know of humans except the love I had shown him? Could I ever find the right place for him? Part of me didn't want to. But as he plopped another poop to the bottom of the pool, I tried to strengthen my resolve.

I continued my search. One place seemed too remote, too wild, the change too extreme. Another was too people-infested. I didn't trust the average human to be kind to his friendly nature. Other places had too many ducks already. Some had too few. I was too-tooing everything, and the days were going by.

"I'm going to set up that acid wash in the next couple of weeks," Mike said, returning from the backyard and his nightly inspection of the pool's dismal condition. "How's the search coming along?"

I started my too-too this and too-too that.

He interrupted my excuses. "Where is Dave? I didn't see him in the yard."

"He's out flying. I expect he'll be back any time now."

At that moment the doorbell rang.

It was a neighbor from down the street. "Are you the duck lady?" he asked.

Mike stifled a chuckle.

"I guess I am," I said.

"Well your duck is down at the end of the cul-de-sac. He seems lost."

"Oh, thanks. He has a hard time landing in our yard. He's new to flying," I explained. "Dave, Dave," I called in my singsong way.

"Wwraack-wwrack-wwrack!" He waddled hard and fast up the road towards us.

"Where have you been, you silly boy?" I scolded him as I bent to pet the chocolate feathers on his chest. "Come on, you must be hungry. Let's go home."

Dave and I started up the driveway, chattering back and forth in Duck, leaving the neighbor, saucer-eyed and aghast.

wwraak
wwraak
wwraak

There was a time when I would not have spoken to Dave like that in the presence of a stranger, afraid of being mocked or laughed at. But I didn't care anymore. I was proud of my duck and grateful for the intimacy that we had created together. As we approached the house I could heard the man say, "I can't believe it; she's like Snow White or something!"

My husband's hearty laugh echoed in the street.

I got a handful of cornflakes and led Dave out into the backyard. Slumping into the patio chair we always shared, I patted my knee. He fluttered soft as a butterfly into my lap and nudged my hand open with his beak. As he crunched away at the flakes I laid my head back and looked into the early evening sky. The odd sadness that had come to light on New Years Day and then faded over the last few months began a fluorescent hum inside me again.

"You two are something else. You blew that guy away."
Mike plopped down on the chair beside me and reached
over to stroke Dave's back feathers. "He went home
scratching his head, said he'd never seen anything like it."
I just looked at him.

"What's the matter?"

"It's so hard to let Dave go."

He sat back, his smile fading, "I know."

And as if to punctuate the inevitable, Dave fluttered
from my lap.

Mike and I sat in silence, holding hands, watching him
as he slipped gracefully into the pool to make his rounds in
the sun's slow setting.

Chapter Five
Separation

I finally decided on a new home for Dave.

It was a small man-made pond nestled in the middle of a light industrial park, about fifteen miles from our home. There was a large stand of pine trees not unlike those in our own backyard with benches where employees could sit during lunch breaks. I counted seven mallards living there. Dave would make it a nice even eight.

"So we can visit him there," Dan said.

"Yes."

"That's good then, Mom. People around that place must like ducks, so he'll be safe," Mitch added.

"Yeah, it's good."

Mike was silent, rubbing his index finger through his mustache, like he always does when he's thinking hard on something.

Two days later the pool was being emptied, but I still hadn't gathered the courage to take Dave to his new home. He left the yard that morning to fly like he did every day since he found his wings. But this time he didn't return. I could only imagine that the empty pool must have looked different to him from the air, that he didn't recognize our yard as he had seen it from above before. I combed the cul-de-sac several times a day in the hope that he would land there. He never did. Instead, as the days went by I began to get telephone calls from around the neighborhood with "Dave sightings." He had landed in a yard or stopped in for a swim in someone's pool; our old babysitter's mother called to say that she had fed him some bread. I had no idea that so many people knew about our duck.

Knowing that he was fine gave us some consolation, but it was not enough. The boys were sorry that they didn't have the chance to say a proper farewell to this duck that had become their brother. Mike was angry with himself for not waiting to empty the pool. And I was despondent, furious at my own reluctance to let Dave go, for not having the courage to end our time together as I had intended – to tenderly release him to that lovely pond, watch him join the other mallards in soft quacks of greeting. I had short-changed our parting.

It seemed impossible that he would return to the now very unfamiliar landscape. After the duck poop could not be extracted from the plaster with the acid wash, we began a full-scale pool renovation, jack hammering out the plaster, which led to tile replacement, which led to the deck replacement. Not once did my husband blame Dave for the cost. Maybe he held back his comments out of respect for my grief. Maybe he felt his own kind of sadness. His only response was, "That plaster was getting old anyhow."

Nearly a month passed. I was on my way home one day, turning onto the street that runs along a small park near my house. Every couple of weeks the basin of the park filled with irrigation water, which made a temporary, shallow lake. I spotted a lone mallard paddling a small wake in the glassy water. I slammed on my brakes. In all the years I'd lived there I had never seen a duck in the park. Everything in me knew it was Dave.

I could hardly contain myself. I sped home, grabbed some bread and cornflakes from the kitchen and ran to the park.

"Dave, Dave," I called. He paddled his way in serpentine fashion to the makeshift shore, talking in low guttural quacks. But he would come no closer. I sat and talked to him, returning the sounds in my best Duck and offering bits of food.

We carried on our conversation for some time. I expressed my regret about the way we had parted and that it was my fault for wanting to keep him too long. Then, as if knowing that I could easily start into a sentimental monologue about him and me, he fluttered into flight, his wings rising and falling in a slow rhythmic movement, circling over the trees. And then he was gone.

I sat staring into the late afternoon sky as it faded from turquoise to hints of gray-blue, scanning the horizon for his return. Finally, I rose and made my way home.

Chapter Six
Transformation

Almost every day Mike would say something like …

"Anybody call about Dave today?"

"Nope," I'd say.

"It's okay, Plynn, he'll show up again."

"Yeah, maybe," I'd say.

"But I sure don't miss the poop. Do you?"

"No, I don't miss the poop."

It was late June. About six weeks had passed since our last meeting at the irrigation lake, and I had developed a habit of scanning the area for Dave.

One day I noticed that, once again, water filled the basin of the park. I slowed my car to a turtle crawl. There by the side of the lake stood a male mallard. I squeaked with glee. But wait … I squinted hard … he wasn't alone. A few feet from his side a female waddled, head down, feeding in the muddy grass of the lakeside.

Once again I sped home, grabbed some bread and cornflakes and sprinted to the park. I stood beside a tree some distance away and watched the pair for a while. Just the two of them on the lake, they paddled in serene unison, dipping their heads in the water, feeding on the lake's temporary ecosystem. It was so quiet in those moments. As I watched I could hear my own breath go in and out, in and out. And with each breath my heart seemed to settle deeper into peace.

I approached the water's edge with careful steps, speaking in low, guttural sounds, "Wraaaack, wraack, wraack," the intimate sounds familiar to Dave and me. He returned my call and paddled toward me, his partner following behind him. I crouched down and tossed bits of food toward them. They duck-muttered as they ate, and I imagined Dave saying to her, "It's okay. She's safe. She's the one I was telling you about." I muttered with them, hoping to make her feel comfortable.

I threw the food closer and closer to the shore until they were both completely out of the water. Dave drew near – almost near enough for me to stroke his back feathers as I once had. Every fiber of my being wanted to, but I didn't. A delicate balance hovered in the air and I would, for certain, ruin all of it if I tried to go back to what once had been.

Instead, I sat and took in what had come into being – Dave, with his iridescent, bottle green neck, long and strong atop the narrow collar of white feathers, his chocolate brown chest, broad and proud, under a topcoat of battle gray. Blue-black, tail feathers sparked with a dapper, white curl. He watched over his mate with such care. As she shuffled along the edge of the lake away from me, picking for food here and there, he moved with her. Never more than a few feet separated them.

I watched, silent and smiling, proud as any mother could be. And then, as if by instinct, I rose to my feet. Dave stopped feeding in the shallow, grassy water and looked at me. I spoke soft and low, "She is beautiful. Thank you for letting me meet her. Thank you..."

"Wraaack, wraack, wraack," he whispered.

We stood there taking each other in for a moment. Then I turned away and walked up the embankment towards home. When I knew I would lose sight of the pair, I took one last look. They had left the shore and were paddling side-by-side across the lake, two V-shaped shimmering wakes intersecting in the still water behind them.

EPILOGUE
Visitation

At least two years had passed since I'd last seen Dave.

Mitch had moved out, was attending college and building his own life on his own terms. Dan was still at home, in his junior year of high school, dreaming about his future and doing his best to wean me, and Mike, from him. We were doing our best to comply.

One early spring morning, the sun barely breathing its way into the hazy gray sky, I shuffled around the kitchen waiting for the coffee to brew. Mike had left for work long before I woke, and Dan was still asleep. Something or nothing moving outside caught my attention. I leaned on the counter that looked through to the family room and out the big picture window into the backyard. A gentle ripple edged its way across the glassy water in the swimming pool.

Oh no, I thought, another baby bird. Dozens of bird families live in the pine trees scattered throughout our yard, and every spring the young try their first flights from the limbs, fluttering helter-skelter to the ground and the perils of skulking kitties, or to the pool and certain watery death. I always made it my mission to rescue as many of them as possible from either demise.

I went to the window, ready to shake off my morning stiffness and run to recover one more soggy bird. I looked out; my hands came to my mouth in a silent gasp. Two mallards stood at the far end of the pool – a male and a female.

"Dave," I whispered.

I didn't know what to do. I bounced back and forth like a

boxer: go out, stay in, get the camera, get Dan. Who would ever believe this? I decided to wake Dan, eased away from the window, and tiptoed through the family room and down, what seemed like, the very long hallway to his bedroom. I touched his arm, got close to his face and spoke in a low, sibilant voice, "Danny. Dave is here."

"What?" He had that vacant look, eyes bleary, jaw slack.

"It's Dave. Dave and his wife are in the backyard. They're standing by the pool. What should we do?" I had completely lost my senses.

Dan leapt out of bed. "Let me see, I want to see them."

"Wait. Let me get the camera." I whispered. Dan followed me to my room. We bumped into each other like two bungling burglars and started to giggle.

Dan put his finger to his lips, "Shhh."

We tiptoed down the hall, through the family room to the back door and stood there in our pajamas, like two small children, peering out the window. They were still there. Dave looked regal and confident. It was as if he were saying, "See, this is where I grew up."

"Let's go out, mom."

Though we tried to ease the door open without a sound, within a moment the pair were in flight, swooping across the pool and up past the pine trees. Dan ran out into the yard, face to the sky, "Dave! Dave! Come back, Dave!"

I stood frozen, camera in hand. Dan looked at me, his young man's face dissolving into the disappointment of the little boy I knew so well. We gathered into a fierce hug. I laid my head on my son's chest; his heart beat in quick, strong thumps. We stood holding one another and stared at the spot the mallards had graced only moments before. Two plops of poop were all that remained.

Our laughter rose up, past the pine trees, into the crisp spring air, into the wide morning blue of the sky.

My Dave

About the Author

Much of Plynn Gutman's creative inspiration has come from the natural world. In addition to Dave the Duck's deep influence in her life, several other animal friends have captured her heart and made their way onto the pages of her poems and stories ~ like one of her beloved cats, Lucius, a poem in West Wind Review 2011, and Sarah the Chicken in the University of Guelph, Ontario Veterinary College's 150th Anniversary Anthology, Animal Companions, Animal Lovers, Animal Doctors.

Plynn's writing has appeared in numerous literary journals over the past twelve years and she is the author of a memoir about her maternal grandmother, *The Work of Her Hands: A Prairie Woman's Life in Remembrances and Recipes*, the e-version memoir of *My Son Dave (the Duck)* and *Your Journal Companion: 365 Writing Prompts to Heighten Awareness of Self and Others*.

Plynn is the owner and facilitator of Your Liminal Space Retreats and has a private practice as an Integrated-Life Coach and Energy Practitioner. Of course, she loves animals of every size, shape and specie, and is deeply dedicated to her husband, two sons and two lovely cats. A transplanted Canadian, Plynn makes her home in Arizona, USA.

Contact: plynngutman@gmail.com
www.plynnsworld.com

Follow Plynn Gutman on Social Media
www.facebook.com/PlynnGutman
www.twitter.com/PlynnGutman

About the Illustrator

Jessica Lynn Woodson, born in Phoenix, Arizona, lived in St. Louis for 10 years before returning to reside in Mesa, Arizona, where she graduated from Mountain View High School in 2001 and went on to receive a Bachelor's Degree in drawing at Arizona State University in 2006. Jessica currently lives in Los Angeles, California where she enjoys creating watercolor paintings for her online Etsy store "The Desert Moon" and is a professional graphic designer for Sony Pictures Entertainment.

Contact: Jessicalynnwoodson@gmail.com
www.etsy.com/shop/thedesertmoon

www.ingramcontent.com/pod-product-compliance
Lightning Source LLC
LaVergne TN
LVHW010022070426
835508LV00001B/7